MY SIDE OF THE STORY

MONOLOGUES FOR TEENS

KRISTIN KAY RASMUSSEN

Printed in the United States of America

First Printing, 2018

ISBN-13: 978-1724721792

ISBN-10: 1724721798

Inquiries can be sent by visiting www.krisrasmussen.net

CONTENTS

AUTHOR'S NOTE

I am in my second decade of teaching and the daily drama of the classroom never ceases to inspire me as a playwright. It's the little murmurings when they don't think I am listening, or the moments that I haven't been able to shake years later that have provided a starting point for many of the moments in this collection.

I wanted to try something for my first collection that would be different than other monologue books I have read. I began experimenting with writing monologues in pairs. (Well, in one occasion, in triplet.) Some of these monologues tell the same event from the perspective of two different characters. Some of them take a turning point, but explore how two characters can react differently. In a beginning drama class, this can be especially helpful if students are not ready just yet for scene study. Students don't have to practice with a partner, but they can still experience the idea of hearing the point of view of one – or more – characters involved in the story. Other monologues tackle the same topic, but from different points of view. This can be its own valuable lesson in character motivation, negotiation of an object, sense memory, and other dramatic principles. (*However, there is nothing about these monologues that precludes them from being stand-*

alone pieces, so I hope I have given teachers and actors as much flexibility as possible.)

As a teacher, I also know that we all appreciate a little extra for our hard-earned money. That's why you'll find rubrics for scoring performances in the back of the book as well as some ideas for lessons. For example, I have included some original writing prompts to inspire students to write one of their own monologues.

Lastly, this book is the first in a series. My hope is to publish a new batch of monologues every six months. Each collection will have a different twist or focus on a different audience. The next collection will focus on monologues specifically for diverse voices.

Happy performing. I love feedback. Feel free to drop me a comment or sign up for my newsletter at www.krisrasmussen.net.

Best wishes,

Kris Rasmussen

PART I
TWO SIDES TO EVERY STORY

BREAK UP? TAKE 1

(*F/COMEDIC*)

Sure. Take her to prom. Good plan. She's hot. And hey, she's dated everyone else in our grade, so why not you? But here's why that's not going to happen. You have a research paper due next week in World History, don't you? Have you started it yet? And it's just sitting there on my laptop. Waiting for me to finish it. No. But I have. Your paper currently has about 1,260 words of information all correctly cited. Maybe I will write the other 1,840. Or not.

But go ahead. It's fine. Take your Kardashian look-alike to the prom.Wikipedia your Russian Revolution research paper and maybe Rogers won't notice…this time.

Oh, wait…there's also that unit test on *Frankenstein* in what…three days? Yeah, I bet you still think Frankenstein is the *doctor*. I took the time to copy the summary from three different websites for you. Plus, I may have told our "special" friend, Cody, I'd go out with him if he would stop by Mrs. Patton's room and get a copy of the test. So…pick me up at six. And don't worry, after prom is over, *I* will break up with *you*.

BREAK UP? TAKE 2

(*M/COMEDIC*)

You are still my prom date. Yes, you are. You are. You will be my date…we just won't be going to the prom…together. I am sorry it has to be this way. If I wasn't taking English 3 for the second time…if I'd bothered to read a book after the fifth grade…we'd so be going. But she's been doing my homework for me all year – which, trust me, is the only reason I started going out with her – and I can't just totally dump her. I've got two assignments for her to turn in still.

But *you* are my date. My real date. You're just the date I am going to meet *at* the prom. That's not that big of a deal, right? I show up with… no, I will not even say her name out loud, that is how much I despise her. I will walk in the door with *her*, take a picture with her in that stupid Gatsby-themed photo booth, and that's it. I am yours, the rest of the night. I swear.

Of course…unless…you know anything about Frankenstein? Or the Russian Revolution? I didn't think so. If you did…if you could write a tiny little history paper for me…and read a few chapters of some crazy book…then I could most definitely ditch her before prom and you could be my prom date the whole time. What? Why won't you help me?

If you can't help me...maybe I'll break up with *you* after prom. I'm kidding. It's a joke. I'll go to summer school. Come back.

(*chases after girlfriend*)

BREAK UP? TAKE 3

(F/COMEDIC)

What? What????? Oh, no, you are taking me to prom. You are. You are. Yes, you are. I bought my dress last September. I know we weren't dating back then. But I knew we would be. I have been in love with you since sixth grade. I have seven diaries devoted to our romance and one of those diaries was just about going to prom. Why are you looking at me like that?

(begins with the tears, eventually working up a real tantrum)

You can take World History over again. And I don't care who this Frankenstein person is. But right now I am only one of five freshman even going to prom. And if I can find a way to break up Ben and Serena, Luke and Katie, and come on, Carrie and Jason have no chance of staying together three more weeks, so, seriously, I can be one of *two* freshman going to the prom. That hasn't happened since 2012.

So you are taking me to prom. And it's going to be amazing. But don't worry. After prom is over, I am breaking up with *you.*

CONCUSSION, TAKE 1

(M/DRAMATIC)

(*Author's note: This monologue can be easily adjusted for football, soccer, or other contact sports.*)

(*athlete, maybe in uniform, leaning against a hockey stick, talking to teammate*)

"I'm fine. Don't worry about me."

(*slams the hockey stick into the wall or the ground for emphasis*)

I kept telling him that and he wouldn't listen. I put three fingers in front of my face. I named the day of the week, the president, my birthday.

(*slams stick, talking to teammate again*)

See. I am fine. Don't say a word. (*threatening*) We're down by one. Greg, I am not kidding.

He skated away. I reached out to grab him and I fell. And he fell. I pulled myself up, I was gonna climb right over him, but I fell again. I wasn't dizzy. I wasn't. I saw the coach coming toward me. It was too late. He's gonna pull me out of the game. But then I saw Greg wasn't getting up. He had taken his helmet off when he was fighting with me.

(*slams the stick*)

Greg...he has headaches now. He hasn't been in school in a few days. Just because he was looking out for me.

(*slams a stick one last time*)

CONCUSSION, TAKE 2

(*M/DRAMATIC*)

(*Greg, young man, possibly in athletic jersey, but sitting down. Tries to read a book. It physically hurts. Puts book down.*)

(*to teammate*) Look at me. Look at me. Dude, you can't focus. You are not okay.

(*to himself*)

I could've believed him. He could remember his name, count the fingers in front of his face. Fine. Let's get back to the game. But he looked in the crowd and I just didn't...he didn't seem like he was really seeing people, you know? And he got pounded last week when we played Central. And last year...he did have a concussion in the district finals. So...I'm his friend. I...just have to do this. I skated over to tell Coach to take him out, but he grabbed my jersey. I don't remember the next moment.

I'm getting better. But I have been out of school for two weeks. And Josh doesn't even bring me my homework assignments. Glad you've got my back, man. Because if I ever get on the ice again, I'll make sure no one has yours.

I LOVE YOU, JOHN GREEN, TAKE 1

(F/COMEDIC)

(teen girl speaking into a camera/phone)

Okay, John Green, I know this is like my twenty-ninth video I have sent you, but if I send you just one more after this one then I will have achieved my goal of making this unofficially I Love You John Green Month, which for some reason Mrs. K is actually giving me extra credit for, and she never allows extra credit, so she probably loves you almost as much as I do. But not quite as much.

I don't even love you because of your novels. I mean, they're great, but I am not one of those girls who argues about which is better – *The Fault in our Stars* or *Looking for Alaska*. But I fell in love with you watching you talk about *The Great Gatsby* on YouTube because I was trying to avoid reading the book. But then just listening to you describe Gatsby and Daisy made me want to read the book and you just have no idea how amazing that is. Then I started watching every YouTube video you've done about all kinds of books I am going to have to read in high school.

So if you're watching this, John Green, and, you have to, you just have to, I love you. And now I realize I can make myself smart enough to find someone just like you to love me. Unless you get divorced like most people do, then I want it to be you. I am sure I'll have graduated from college by then. Okay, forget I said that. No, don't. Because I really do love you. See you tomorrow.

I HATE YOU, JOHN GREEN, TAKE 2

(*m/comedic*)

(*Author's note: Nicholas Sparks and* The Notebook, Dear John, *etc. could work just as well as a substitute in this speech.*)

(*boy speaking into a camera*)

Hey, John Green!

I hate you. Bet you don't hear that much these days, do you? But I hate you. Yeah, my girlfriend is obsessed with you and it's ruining my life. I don't just mean that she loves your books and has read all of them at least ten times. Because she has. I will sit through *The Fault in our Stars* as many times as she wants, I swear. But the fast, quippy way you talk? I can't do that. Self-deprecating anecdotes? Don't have that many. And your insanely large vocabulary that you make sound so cool? Well, *I* just sound like an idiot when *I* use big words like "esoteric" or "ostensibly."

She also loves the way you talk about fatherhood and I am sixteen, man, and I am trying to be responsible, okay? I hate you because you have made it impossible for me to live up to her expectations of what a boyfriend should be. And I do want to be a good boyfriend because my girlfriend, she is the best. But I am not going to be the guy to get the matching *Paper Towns* tattoo with his girlfriend as a declaration of love. So help me out. Make your next book about zombies, aliens – not vampires, though – and the girl and the guy have realllllly low expectations of each other. She'll never read that. Thanks.

SANDWICH, TAKE 1

(*M/F SERIO-COMIC*)

Is this the detention room? Great. What do I do here? I am not – I just – I don't know. Where do I sit? My homework is all done, but I brought a book to read.

No, I am sure I am supposed to be here. Because I shared food with a kid who hasn't eaten in two days and it's against the policy of this school to share food at lunch. Yeah, I bet you didn't know that, did you? I did. I memorize the handbook the first week of school every year, and I understand the theoretical logic behind the rule, but you know the kid is new to the school. I don't know anything about him, but I can tell he's hungry. He has no food in front of him but he is drooling over everyone else's mystery meat. So I broke the rule. First time since kindergarten.

So my mom made me another Caprese sandwich with a side of avocado guacamole egg salad. One day, I would love just a tuna fish sandwich, please, so I gave the kid the guacamole egg salad. Not that big of a loss. I also shared my eggplant fries with marinara sauce for dipping. He wasn't such a big fan of that, but ate it anyway. Now I realize giving someone eggplant does look like I could be wishing them harm, but I wasn't. If I was *allowed* potato chips and Go-Gurt for lunch, I would have given him that, too.

14

You want me to leave? Why? That would be breaking the rules. Good idea, give me another detention.

SANDWICH, TAKE 2

(M/F SERIO-COMIC)

Day one at my new school and they give me a translator because they assume I can't say more than hello or goodbye. Just because I have had to change schools five times already this year doesn't mean there aren't school records somewhere that would tell them I can speak your language even if my parents can't.

I play along because it's easier, but by lunch time it was *"¿Dónde está el baño?"* and I ditch the translator on the way to the bathroom and head to the cafeteria. I am so hungry. But I have no money. I know no one. I sit down in a corner by a window, but then this kid comes over to me and sits down. Talks to me in English. Hands me the weirdest looking food ever. But I don't want to be rude, you know, so I eat it all. And the kid gives me some more. And I eat all of it. And then the lunch monitor comes over and tells him to go to the office. He got detention for giving me food because it's a school rule not to share food. So I think I am going to go to class and swear in Spanish and see if I can get detention and hang out with my new friend.

GERMS, TAKE 1

(M/SERIO-COMIC)

(an older brother, Jake, is swinging a bat and practicing hitting a ball)

Go in the house if you're not gonna play, you wuss. Afraid you're gonna get some germs on you? *Go* inside and find the bacteria wipes for your diaper rash, you baby.

(hits the ball to his brother, winces)

Catch the ball!!!! Do not cry to mom. You're fine. Seriously, don't even think of crying. Just stay out here, okay? I'll help you.

(wipes the ball off)

Okay, it's clean. Ish. No micro whatever you call 'em. Now try again. I am doing you a favor. Come on, try it once.

(throws ball)

Well, you didn't flinch as much that time. Now pick the ball up and throw it back to me. You can do it.

(ball is coming at him, he must duck)

You didn't have to throw it that hard.

Hey, you threw the ball hard. And you didn't throw up! Dude, you aren't going to grow up to be a loser. Now catch this, you twit.

(throws as hard as he can one last time)

Oops. Sorry. Never forget I am always better than you.
(walks off laughing)

GERMS, TAKE 2

(*m/serio-comic*)

(*a boy with a glove holding a baseball as if it is glass, or holding a baseball bat as if it is poison*)

I am doing this. I am holding the ball. I am doing this. I am going to make the team. I am doing this.

(*the boy tosses the ball in the air repeatedly*)

I am catching this ball. There are no pathogenic microorganisms on this ball that can harm me. There are no filamentous organisms on this ball that can infect me.

(*boy stops tossing the ball*)

Yeah, Jake, I am gonna throw the ball, just give me a sec. I can throw the ball. I will throw the ball just like I practiced with mom...

(*deep breath*)

Okay, Jake, get ready.

(*throws the ball*)

Wow.

Sorry, Jake. Does it hurt? Good!

(*sees the ball coming back at him*)

No, don't throw it back. It might have mutant bacteria on it!

(ducks)
I can pick up the baseball. I can do it.
(he almost does it, then runs off stage)

BULLY? TAKE 1

(F/DRAMATIC)

Let's start with my brother peed out the window during first hour because he thought the sub wouldn't notice. So now he is what – suspended, expelled over a stupid prank? And if I hadn't been late for the 36th time this semester, I might have been able to stop that, or if he told me he was gonna try it, I would have punched him and said, don't be a moron. But I *was* late. Yeah, Mom's boyfriend kicked me out last night so I had to sleep in my truck in my boyfriend's driveway. Yeah, his mom won't let me in the house – because she thinks *that's* gonna stop us.

So yeah, I wasn't too happy when I was just walking down the hall to Kennedy's class and Taylor bumped into me. And it was on purpose. *Again.* So I said, let's do this. I know you cheated on Hunter and he is a friend of my boyfriend's so he's my friend, too, and I didn't really appreciate it. So when she told me she didn't give a... Yeah, that was it. I pushed her and we were right by the stairs on the north wing...and she slipped and fell. She didn't dare get up, so, okay, I guess that makes me a bully. Yeah. I guess it does. But now you know why. And she's gonna be fine, right? Right?

BULLY? TAKE 2

(F/DRAMATIC)

(to a friend)

My ankle is probably sprained. I probably won't be able to come to school tomorrow. Maybe not even the rest of the week. My mom is gonna go after her mom so hard, you have no idea. Yeah. Bet she's gonna press charges. I didn't even do any of the things Laura said I did. I don't bump into her on purpose in the halls because she smells. I don't hang out with her boyfriend or friends of her boyfriend because I don't want to catch a disease. I might have called her a name, but that doesn't mean she gets to push me. Pushed me so hard that me, all-conference in soccer and volleyball, oops, fell all the way down the stairs.

(winces)

Ouch. I think I am feeling worse. Here, this is a good shot for Instagram, right? Perfect. Thanks. Here comes Mr. Holt. Let's tell him what happened to me, okay?

THE VEST, TAKE 1

(*M/SERIO-COMIC*)

    (*male, admiring a hideous uniform vest*)

    This vest, this vest is my superpower.

    (*takes a good whiff of the fabric*)

    It smells like popcorn butter no matter how many times Mom washes it. It's supposed to be one size fits all, but... (*tugs at it and shrugs*) And, yes, the color reminds me of something you'd find in a baby's diaper. Everything amazing that has ever happened to me has happened while wearing this vest.

    My first paycheck from Sterling Seven Cinemas was enough money for me to buy the new Call of Duty when my mom told me I couldn't have it. Then Sterling Seven Cinema gave me a best friend. Benji Schmidt. He came to see every Marvel movie at least five times. So I stopped him in the lobby and asked if he liked to play Call of Duty. He said he'd rather play Fortnight and he'd teach me how to play. You don't know how surprising it was to be invited to someone's house.

    Still, the best thing that has happened wearing this vest is...I have finally met my first almost-girlfriend. She just started working here. She's always asking me to bring her a soda if she's selling tickets. She pretends she doesn't know how to work the popcorn machine even though I have shown her at least twenty times. She always has a book in her back pocket by somebody I have never heard of.

Oh, she's waving her hands. She probably wants another soda. And then (*deep breath*) …ask if she wants to stay after work, go up to the sound booth and watch the new *Avengers* movie before everyone else sees it.

THE VEST, TAKE 2

(f/serio-comic)

(girl, either hanging onto or wearing a giant, ugly uniform vest, complaining about her first job, bandages on her arms from on-the-job injuries)

I can't wear this vest. It smells like diaper. And it's five sizes too big.

(flaps arms up and down, pretending to get into the vest, but can't, gets frustrated and stops)

All I wanted to do is go to Harry Potter Writing Camp this summer and suddenly my parents decide I need to *earn* my way so I will *appreciate* it. People who are more comfortable reading about magical creatures and working on their first full-length novel that is *not* fan fiction should not be made to work in the customer service industry. I should not be allowed around dangerous equipment that spews molten butter and gives third degree burns.

(rubs her arms, then notices someone staring at her)

Oh, no. He's looking at me again. Why did the manager assign such a cute guy to train me? He's still looking at me. He is probably going to report me for not being in uniform.

(scrambles to put on the vest but also continues to fight with it during the following lines)

He's bringing me another soda. Why does he keep doing that? He's already brought me two super slurps this shift. I avoid sugar. And carbonation. I am bloated, and burping on customers. And I really have to go the bathroom. Do I ask him if I can go the bathroom? That would be so weird next time I see him in the hall at school. Okay, I will just distract myself from needing to go to the bathroom by asking him which *Twilight Zone* episodes I should binge watch tonight. Or ask him why he thinks *Lord of the Rings* is so much better than *Harry Potter*. I mean he's so sweet, but that's crazy to think that.

(finally gets the vest on, tries to paste on a smile, reaches for a super slurp)
Hi. Thanks. I was getting so thirsty.

THE HUNT, TAKE 1

(*F/COMEDIC*)

(*seated at a dinner table*)

No, thank you. (*beat*) I said, no, thank you. I have mashed potatoes, squash, green beans. I am fine.

I am not eating it. (*beat*) No, I am not. But go ahead. Feel free to eat the flesh of the helpless life you slaughtered.

(*pause*)

What were you thinking anyway?

(*imitating Dad*) "I need to spend more time with my daughter. I know. I'll take her out in the freezing cold super early one Saturday morning for a daddy-daughter deer hunt. I hope she doesn't mind I like to murder angelic furry creatures."

Next time just suck it up and realize you should take me to the movies or look over my shoulder while I spend your money on clothes.

THE HUNT, TAKE 2

(*F/SERIO-COMIC*)

   (*crouching down as if in a deer blind or stalking prey from the ground*)

There was blood everywhere. Even a few intestines oozing out. It was amazing. Five years of begging my dad to let me go out deer hunting with him. Two years of safety for junior hunters classes. Finally. I mean, it wasn't a clean hit. But my old man said, "Take the shot." So I did. And the deer fell. I think it was paralyzed. Then it kinda fell over. It was still alive. I looked into my dad's eyes and he said, "Well?" I took a step. Another step. Had to look into those eyes and put a bullet right between them. Then it was dead. All the way dead. I smiled at my dad and he helped me put in it in the back of the truck, and I didn't have to say a word all the way home because Dad couldn't shut up about how proud of me he was.

   I didn't throw up until we got home and I could lock myself in the bathroom. But I'd do it again. I will do it again. Because my dad was so proud of me.

SKINNY GIRL, TAKE 1

(*F/DRAMATIC*)

(*Girl is only slightly heavier than what we would think for someone who is athletic. In fact, the girl may not be heavy at all. She is in workout clothes for gym class and is warming up with a friend, watching a fellow student across the gym floor.*)

(*muttering to self*) Toothpick. Clothes hanger. She is so skinny. Eat a cheeseburger, why don't you?

I haven't eaten bread since eighth grade. No soda since last semester. Never gonna look like that.

(*begins stretching, warming up*)

You're right. She's probably bulimic. I see her ask for a pass to leave the lunchroom almost every day.

(*mimics gagging*)

I can hold a plank longer than her. I bet you could run a mile faster than her. Right. It's about muscle.

Cardio. Not having your ribs stick out.

(*Look of panic crosses her face*)

Oh, no. She's coming over here. She looks angry. She heard us. Right. Maybe she didn't.

(watches as the girl they are talking about walks past)

Is she okay? She didn't look okay, did she? Maybe I should go check on her. You're right. I am sure twiggy doesn't need our help.

SKINNY GIRL, TAKE 2

(*F/DRAMATIC*)

(*Girl sits in a chair shoving her face with food. As she eats, she also fidgets periodically, maybe with a fidget spinner, throughout this speech as someone who has a hard time focusing or sitting still would.*)

(*imitating someone else's mocking voice*) "Why don't you just eat a cheeseburger? You're just sooo skinny."

I *do* eat cheeseburgers. I love cheeseburgers. I love cheesecake. I love *cheese*.

But if I say that, then it's all, "I hate you. You look like *that* and you eat whatever you want."

(*stops eating and pulls a bottle of pills out of her pocket*)

And yet the doctor says I am supposed to keep taking this. Adderall. It helps you focus, Sara. You know you do better in class when you take it, Sara. Just try it for a little while longer, Sara.

I've tried it. Yeah, it also makes it even *harder* for me to gain weight. I don't want to eat when I am on this junk. I throw up sometimes. But at least I'm not using a fidget spinner in class.

(*picks up pill bottle*)

I have to take it. They're going to make me take it.

(opens bottle, take a pill, closes bottle. Long pause, goes back to stuffing her face with food.)

GROUP PROJECT, TAKE 1

(*M/F COMEDIC*)

(*Author's note: This doesn't need to be played aggressive or snarky. Think of it as the character giving this speech as a sign of defeat, a loss of hope.*)

(*student hands out pieces of paper to each student as he/she speaks*)

I have contracts prepared for all of you. As you can see in item 1, line 2, I agree to do 90 percent of the work for this group project, because, well, we have known each other since fifth grade and let's not pretend anymore. However, as noted in line 5, we still will all give each other tens on our group self-evaluations saying that we all contributed equally, in a positive and productive manner.

I will have this project done by six o'clock tonight. I will do the research. I will create the prezi...but because I would rather die than speak in front of thirty students who couldn't care less about what I am saying, you three will present the material. Zane will open with some gross joke that will get everybody's attention and may or may not get him kicked out of class. Colin will present the main ideas because you're intelligent but don't want to try, and Mandy will answer follow up questions, because, well, it's the one thing you should be able to do.

All each of you has to do is look at my presentation before class Thursday and be familiar with the information. Please do not sound like a robot when you present it or stare at the screen like it's the first time you have ever seen the words because the Salem Witch Trials really are fascinating and relevant to the mob mentality in today's society.

(*dead silence, student sighs*)

Just sign the contracts so we can all to lunch, okay?

GROUP PROJECT, TAKE 2

(*M/F COMEDIC*)

(Actor is creating a monument using everyday household items: beans, rice, buttons, etc. Almost at the end of the project, perhaps standing on a stool to give an indication of how large the project is. Places each bean or item used very carefully on the memorial being created. A sibling is helping work on the memorial under great protest.)

Keep gluing. We only have to put on 5,989,682 more to go. Yes, one bean for every life lost in the Holocaust. I don't care. Keep going. I helped you with your Trojan Horse project, which you got an A on, thanks to me. Yeah, it *was* because of me. You cut my hair to use for the horse's tail. And my Holocaust memorial is going to be way better than your Trojan Horse. Six million navy beans representing six million Holocaust survivors. It's an A+.

(continues placing beans)

Okay, it's not really going to be six million. That would take forever. But you know, maybe six thousand...that would be close enough, right? If you stop now, I am telling Mom about what you have hidden in your Batman socks in your bottom drawer. Umm...where are we at...

Hey, what are you doing? Don't let –

(structure collapses)

You did that on purpose. Do not move. We are starting over. If you leave...

(sighs, begins picking up beans, putting them back on memorial)

Fine. I'll do it myself. One, two, three...six hundred. That would be pretty good.

PART II
BONUS MONOLOGUES

THE ORGANIZER

(*M/F COMEDIC*)

(*student entering a classroom at the end of the day, talking to the teacher*)

Can I come in for a sec, Mrs. Cooper? No, I can't retake that vocab quiz right now. I should, you're right, 2 out of 20 is a bad score. I'll take it tomorrow, I swear. I just wanted to ask you a question. Can I reorganize your bookcase?

(*moves to a bookcase and starts rearranging books*)

I was trying to listen to what you were saying about parallel structure last hour. I was writing down the sentence. Billy likes to run, to swim...but some kid put *To Kill a Mockingbird* in your science fiction section. And all I wanted to do is get up and put it in the fiction section. Which is when I noticed three copies of *The Glass Castle* in the science fiction section. How do kids these days not know that is a memoir? They should really pay more attention.

(deep breath) Okay. That looks good, right? Better? Okay. I gotta go. Yes, vocab test. Tomorrow at lunch.

(*starts to leave, turns around*)

I'm sorry. But there's just a smudge over there in the very top corner of the board...do you mind?

(hands up, backs off)
Okay, okay, I am going.

THE MASCOT

(*M/F COMEDIC*)

(*very soft*)

I can go all day without anyone noticing me. I get marked absent more than anyone I know...and I sit in the front row. (sigh) My parents don't always realize I am home and forget to tell me dinner's ready. Or turn the light's off while I am still in the room. I don't mind really. I like the dark.

But Miss Bozman – she *saw* me. Saw me trying to blend into my locker ever morning by pretending I was looking for a missing homework assignment. She knew I was late to third hour all the time just so I could get lunch detention and eat my cheese sandwich *alone*. Then she called me to her office and gave me the tiger costume. She wanted me to be the new mascot for the Madison High School Tigers.

(*motions put on costume, voice now grows in strength, but it is still pretty meek*)

ROOAARR

It felt really good.

(again a little louder)

ROOOAAARRR

(louder)

ROOOAAARRR

And now I am the school mascot. My first game is tonight. Nobody knows it's going to be me, Miss Bozman promised.

(one final epic sound)

ROOOAAARRRRRR!!!!!!!!!!!!!!

RECRUIT

(*m/dramatic*)

(*guy runs on stage singing a marine song, runs in place for a moment as he sings*)

"We fight our country's battles, on the land and on the sea
First to fight for right and freedom and to keep our honor clean"

(*stops to begin some push ups, then continues song*)

"We are proud to claim the title of United States Marine."

(*stretches*)

I got my three-mile run down to 22 minutes. YES! New personal best. I can do 50 crunches in two minutes. U.S. Marines, here I come.

(*pulls a letter up out of his pocket*)

Say bye-bye, University of Michigan medical school.

(*tears the letter up*)

First to *not* go to college, so OOHRAH THAT, GRANDPA, from your grandson, Wideload. No medical school for me, OOHRAH, DAD. Keep your family practice for some other family member named Tubby Tard. Time to be proud of me for me. Going to Iraq, Afghanistan, North Korea, everywhere the U.S. wants me, man, on my way to being an officer at the Pentagon. Officer at the Pentagon, and I won't ever put your name on the list to visit me. OOHRAH.

Okay, three more miles. I can beat that time like I am gonna beat my enemies! OOHRAH!

(*sings as he runs off*)

"We fight our country's battles, on the land and on the sea

First to fight for right and freedom and to keep our honor clean"

CONFERENCES

(*M/F COMEDIC*)

Mamá, esta mi profesor de Inglés Sra. Williams. Mrs. Williams, my mother. I feel stupid, this is supposed to be a parent-teacher conference, but my mother doesn't speak English, so I get to be here. I don't know why she won't learn to speak English. Five years here and she won't even try.

¿Por qué no aprender a hablar Inglés mamá? Ella dice que soy un excelente estudiante.

Oh, you think you understood most of that? Are you sure? Well, come on, I am pretty good in class most of the time right, Mrs. Williams? Oh, Mrs. Williams, don't make me tell her that…please? Okay, I'll tell her. Mama, I did not turn my essay on Great Gatsby in. I think she understood that. It's a miracle. (*beat*)

Mamá, Mamá, no me dirijo en mi ensayo sobre la Grand Gatsby.

I just lost my cell phone for the rest of the week, Mrs. Williams. Thanks. Thanks a lot.

COFFEE TABLE

(M/DRAMATIC)

There's a knock on the front door. I always tell Andrew not to not knock. Just come in and bring whatever little...gift...he has for me. I open the door. It's not Andrew. It's Mr. Mancini. New chemistry teacher. A teacher at my house. What the...? And I tell Pops I got it...and he doesn't need to come in, just stay in the kitchen. So I try to not act too weird, and ask Mancini, what is he doing here, did he get lost, doesn't he have a life. He doesn't say a word. He just walks over to the coffee table. He touches it. He rubs his hand over it. I am really trying not to creep out.

Then he says, "You wrote on one of the desks today. With a Sharpie. And it wasn't school appropriate."

SO? I did five other things worse than that before lunch. But then Pops comes into the room and Mancini introduces himself, pulls out a Sharpie, and asks Pops if he would mind if he drew s picture on the coffee table. Dad tells him to get out using all of the swear words he can slur. So Mancini tells Pops what I did. I think Pops is gonna laugh in Mancini's face. But instead Pops stops swearing and says, "I see your point. Sure, write on our coffee table. My son will buy us a new one."

Mancini looks me in the eyes. He puts the Sharpie away. Shakes Pop's hand and walks out. Mancini and I have been best buds ever since.

PURPLE

(*M/F DRAMATIC*)

Everyone is wearing purple because someone said it's Jared's favorite color. I don't remember him wearing purple once. People are lining up in the cafeteria…writing sappy crap on some roll of paper…you always made me laugh…I'll miss your smile. Jared never cracked a joke and was too busy drawing skulls all over his notebook to smile.

My father's favorite color is brown. I can't even get him to wear navy blue. Just brown. Not that anyone is asking.

No one knows he can't get out of bed. No one thinks it's his fault, what happened to Jared, but no one asks about him either. Or about me. Or my mom. He was just doing his job. Throwing garbage in the back of the truck. He wasn't even behind the wheel when the car slid into the truck. He could have been hurt, too, you know. Maybe he could have died and I wouldn't have a dad. Or maybe if it had happened two minutes later, he would have been at the next house and it wouldn't have happened at all.

But I can't say any of that. All I can do is wear purple. And cry. And people don't really know why.

HALL PASS

(*m/f COMEDIC*)

I have not used all of my passes. No, I have not. (*turning to classmates*) Guys? Have I used all of my passes?

Shut up, Robert.

(*back to teacher*) See, everyone knows I haven't used all of my passes.

(*switches tactics*) Look, I am sick. I can't help it if I am sick, right?

You don't want me to throw up in the trash can, do you?

And I really am. I am gonna puke. (dry heaves, possibly) That was close.

Not to mention... (*mouths the words "diarrhea" or possibly "female problems"*)

(*beat, switches tactics*)

Okay, call Mrs. Moore. I was supposed to go down and meet with her about my schedule for next semester. I'll get a pass from her, okay?

(*beat, switches tactics*)

Okay, I have used up all my passes. And I shouldn't have lied. I'll come in at lunch and clean the desks. I'll come in after school and clean the board. Okay, I will say it. I'm bored and I don't really have to go.

(*beat*)

Now can I have a pass?
Sits down

SNOW DAY

(M/F SERIO-COMIC)

(teen is bundled in a blanket, maybe clutching a pillow, shivering, looks at phone or TV set intently, waiting for something)

Come on. Come on. Not us. Not us. Pppleeeeassee, not us. NOOOOOO.

(punches a pillow)

Today is gonna suck.

(yelling to someone in the next room.)

I know. I know. There's no school. Go back to sleep.

(big sigh, tries to go back to sleep, interrupted by voices in the next room again)

(yelling into next room) We don't have any cereal. Go back to bed. You ate the last of the peanut butter last night. Go back to bed.

(punches pillow, reminisces)

Snow days haven't been fun since I was...ten. (sigh) Those were the days. It was just me. No step-whatevers. No six-month-old baby. Mom would go to work and I would eat fifty pizza rolls, drink a 2-liter of Mountain Dew, find the leftover candy canes and get sick to my stomach.

(*yelling into the other room again*) Put on an extra sweatshirt. I am cold, too.

Then I would tell Mom it was the flu, and she felt guilty for working all the time, so then she kept me home from school the next day, too. (*sigh of bliss*)

(*to someone in the next room*) I'm going to go shovel the driveway. Then we can walk to the library where it's warm. Okay? They might have hot chocolate and cookies.

(*stands up, throws off blanket and trudges off stage*)

I hate snow days.

EMANCIPATION

(F/DRAMATIC)

(teen girl stands before a judge who is considering her petition to become an emancipated minor)

No, Your Honor, pretty sure neither of my parents are going to be here today to listen to this petition. I don't know where my father is. This time of the year he has usually set up a tent under the bridge, but I haven't checked. It's just me. You can see that I have my own income. I have a job. Two actually. I work at Pepe's Pizza on most weeknights and I clean houses on weekends sometimes.

It's not too much for me. I have a B average. I am sure all As would be more impressive, but I get my work in on time and I hate math, so that hurts the ol' GPA. I have been getting myself to school since I was ten. I even go to parent-teacher conferences. "Mrs. Blah-blah-blah, how am I doing in your class? I am, aren't I? Thanks. Have a nice night, Mrs.Blah-Blah-blah."

Yes, sir, I have a sister in Florida, but I am not moving there. She's got two kids already and she's only two years older than me. I have three semesters of high school left. I want to graduate with my friends, Your Honor. One of my neighbors introduced me to this little old lady, Esther, and she said I can move in. I wouldn't have to pay her rent if I cook meals and do errands and help out around the house. I can do that. I do it now. I just do it for a drug addict with an arrest record who usually steals my paycheck from Pepe's Pizza. Esther smells a little weird and is hard of hearing, but she is probably going to be a nice change of pace, don't you think?

I know you would rather not make this choice, Your Honor. I would rather spend time choosing prom dresses and colleges. I guess I could get pregnant and marry my boyfriend and that would make me legally independent, but that just seems like a really bad choice to me. Ask my sister.

(*beat*)

So if you could just sign that petition.

(*beat*)

Thank you. Thank you, Your Honor.

APPENDIX

Monologue Rubrics

Criteria	Developing	Adequate	Proficient	Excels
Purpose	the purpose of the monologue is confusing and rarely reveals the thoughts, feelings, intentions or context of the character	the monologue occasionally reveals the thoughts, feelings, and context of the character	the monologue interprets the thoughts, feelings intentions, and context of the character	the monologue effectively elaborates the thoughts, feelings, intentions and context of the character
Elements	point of view and person are inconsistent; an implied listener is seldom evident	point of view and person are clear and consistent; an implied listener is evident	point of view and person are clear, focused, and consistent; an implied listener is established	point of view and person are integrated; an implied listener is evident throughout the monologue
Physical Delivery	lacks involvement; no movement or gestures	behaviors, gestures, or movements do not fit the character	gestures or movements are fine, but may have omitted obvious character behaviors	natural gestures and movement enhance message; fit character or role
Speaking	Almost no variety in volume, tone, and pace limited or no use of nonverbal gestures and facial expressions	uses volume, tone, and pace somewhat to suit the content and purpose;	uses volume, tone, and pace appropriate to the content and purpose; nonverbal gestures and facial expression suit the character	There is a variety of volume, tone, and pace to create emphasis and enhance the performance;
Knowledge of Script	is not able to perform without script	needs constant prompting to perform	is able to perform with little prompting	is able to perform successfully with no prompting

Delivery	Not Yet Within Expectations (1-2)	Minimally Meets Expectations (3)	Fully Meets Expectations (4)	Exceeds Expectations (5)
Point of View	• point of view and character are inconsistent • an implied listener is seldom evident	• point of view and character are clear and consistent • an implied listener is evident	• point of view and character are clear, focused, and consistent • an implied listener is established	• point of view and character are integrated; • an implied listener is evident throughout the monologue
Physical Delivery	• lacks involvement; no movement or gestures • limited use of nonverbal gestures and facial expressions	• behaviors, gestures, or movements do not fit the character • nonverbal gestures and facial expressions are occasionally distracting or inappropriate for the character	• gestures or movements are fine, but may have omitted obvious character behaviors • nonverbal gestures and facial expression suit the character	• natural gestures and movement enhance message; fit character or role • nonverbal gestures and facial expression enhance characterization
Pacing	• Either too fast or too slow.	• Either too fast or too slow or length.	• Delivery generally Successful.	• Excellent pacing, including dramatic pauses.
Speaking Techniques	• uses volume, tone, and pace inappropriately or ineffectively • Enunciation is not clear; monologue does not flow smoothly and contains many breaks or fillers that are out of character	• uses volume, tone, and pace somewhat to suit the content and purpose • Enunciation is mostly clear; monologue flows adequately with some noticeable breaks or fillers (um, uh, etc.) that are out of character	• uses volume, tone, and pace appropriate to the content and purpose • Enunciation is clear; expression is appropriate and natural; monologue flows well with few noticeable breaks or fillers that are out of character	• adjusts volume, tone, and pace to achieve a special effect or for impact • Enunciation is exceptionally clear; monologue flows smoothly without noticeable breaks or fillers that are out of character

EXTENSION ACTIVITIES

1. Take one of the scenarios from one of the monologues in this book: first hunt, first job, first break-up, group project. Write a monologue by creating a character going through that experience but with different emotions, a different outcome, or speaking to a different character.

2. Write a monologue, but you have to incorporate one of these lines into your monologue.
   A. I forgot to bring it.
   B. That's something I'll never do again.
   C. I can't wear this.
   D. When can you get here?
   E. Why is that for sale?
   F. I told *you* to do it.

3. Pick an object, similar to some of the ones in the monologues: a piece of clothing like a vest, or a piece of food. Now write a monologue around it. How is the piece of clothing important? If you are writing about an object, does someone else want the object? What would they do to get it?

ABOUT THE AUTHOR

Kris Rasmussen is a teacher and a playwright with degrees from Michigan State University and Ferris State University. She has taught in the public school system for twelve years. Her dramatic work has been performed on stage at regional theaters such as the Forward Theater Company in Madison, Wisconsin. Her work has been published by Lillenas Drama. For more information, contact her at www.krisrasmussen.net, on Twitter @krisras63 or on Instagram at kris.ras.

twitter.com/krisras63

instagram.com/kris.ras

CPSIA information can be obtained
at www.ICGtesting.com
Printed in the USA
LVHW080054300722
724710LV00021B/1498

9 781724 721792